ANNI

WHERE DO I GO
FROM HERE?

A Collection of Short Stories Depicting the Journey
of My Soul from the Dark Years into the Light

Published by
Hasmark Publishing
www.hasmarkpublishing.com

Permission should be addressed in writing to Annie Baatz at Anne.Baatz@aol.com.

Editor: Sigrid Macdonald
Book Magic
http://bookmagic.ca

Cover & Book Design: Anne Karklins
annekarklins@gmail.com

ISBN 13: 978-1-989161-56-2
ISBN 10: 1989161561

THANK YOU

I would like to thank my family, especially my sister Joan, for their unconditional support through the darkest times of my life. Their love, concern, and support got me through day by day.

I would like to thank my friends, so many, who encouraged and supported me through these trials and tribulations, my sadness, and darkness.

Bernadette who never gave up on me; her concern for me will stay with me forever. A true and loyal friend.

I would especially like to thank my therapist, Yolanda, who played a large part in where I am today, for her love and support.

Professor David for opening his heart to me and my daughter at a time when our lives were in total chaos.

Thank you most of all to my beautiful daughters for your support throughout these years. We had to learn so much together, be supportive together, cry together. Thank you for allowing me to do what I had to do to support us, and you had to grow up quickly and become so strong and wise. We have come through a lot in these few short years, but what we have overcome together no one can ever take from us. So proud of the ladies you are today! Stay strong and follow your heart.

Thank you to everyone for helping me get where I am today, for giving me courage, and offering me opportunities to step into my authentic self.

Thank you to God and the Universe for always reminding me to see the light and to have hope!

CONTENTS

THE
JOURNEY
OF
THE HEART

PART 1
THE TREASURE CHEST

The pain. Oh, the pain.

The heart feeling such loss, the sadness so deep.

The feeling of being dropped

and breaking into a million pieces

like a glass chandelier.

The disbelief at how this could happen;

the hopelessness of how it could ever be put back together suffocated me.

The hurt, the pain overtook me day after day, month after month, year after year.

The tears continued to flow

like a dam that had burst at the seams

unable to stop.

I made a decision no one would ever get close to me again.

I buried my heart!

I carefully took my heart, and I gently placed it inside a treasure chest,

and I took it to the depths of the ocean.

I found a safe place and buried it there.

Covering it in such a way the murky water, the weeds, the sharks, the eels

always swimming close by

would scare anyone from coming close

and finally slammed the prison doors shut,

the clanging a reminder to stay away.

The loneliness set in, the sadness constantly by my side.

At night, when no one was around, and the pain too unbearable to feel,

I would swim to the bottom of the ocean,

open the prison bars,

swim to the treasure chest,

and ever so delicately pick up my broken heart

and place it in my two hands,

hold it up to God, and say,

"You have to do something with this"

as the tears flowed uncontrollably down my face, my body shaking.

Then I would place it ever so gently back again in the treasure chest.

Bury it.

Slam the prison door shut;

the clanking again the reminder to stay away.

Time after time, when the pain became too much for me to handle,

I would swim again to the bottom of the ocean.

Again, ever so gently, I would place my battered and bruised heart in my two hands,

Hold them up to God and say,

"You have to do something with this!"

This continued again and again!

The friendship I had

Was something I had never experienced.

She was the light in my darkness.

She was the only one I confided in about how unhappy I was with my life and where I was. I felt safe with her; she showed me how to have fun.

I did not have fun in my life for a long time.

She always had time for me; she never judged me. I felt so lucky to have her in my life. I started to feel alive.

I felt I could do anything, get through anything, as long as she was a part of my life.

I could hear the sound of laughter of my own voice, and it felt so good to be accepted for who I was and just be myself.

The relationship began to get strained; the companionship was fading.

There was no communication. I could not understand what was happening. In my meditation, I had an out of body experience. It was as if I were lifted four feet up out of my body, and I looked down and I could see both of us, and I could see my part in contributing to the failure of the friendship. I needed so much, and she could not give me what I needed. She had to protect her space, herself, from all my demands.

The day came when I was told she could no longer be my friend, and our friendship would not continue.

Just that, and no specific reasons given. There was no closure for a long time, but it did come for both of us..

Everything crashed around me. The only true friend I had, the only person I could confide in, was gone.

The pain ripped my heart out. I felt everything drain out of me, my body in shock.

The loss reached the bottom of my soul; it was as if someone reached inside my body and ripped my heart out. I was inconsolable; the mourning of this friendship was unbearable.

My heart feeling such loss, I was inconsolable; the hopelessness of how I could move forward immobilized me. "What will happen to me?"

I was in therapy at this time, and I asked my therapist, "What happened"? at least a million times. I could not hear her for a very long time. She could not reach me; my pain was so deep. I spent one year in therapy focusing on this loss as I was unable to move forward. I was stuck in a dark hole, and I had to feel the unbearable feelings, the loss, the sadness, the mourning. I cried every week in her office for at least a year.

PART 2
THE WATERFALL

As time passed, the sadness was my companion.

Life continued to happen.

My heart became cold.

I could turn to stone in the blink of an eye;

like the turning of a switch, I could build a wall,

protecting outsiders from getting close.

Every year I went on a retreat, a place to grow my inner life, to have space,

to try to find the meaning of life away from my daily routine.

We were walking in the footsteps of St. Francis of Assisi, Italy.

My retreat leader was reading a chapter on love.

I was unable to comprehend one word she was reading.

It was as if she were speaking a different language.

I was so far removed from love.

I was sitting on a rock in the cave where St. Francis went after receiving the Stigmata,

and a Divine Intervention occurred.

A waterfall flowed through my heart.

In that moment, I heard the words love and forgiveness.

And in that moment, I knew God's directions for me was: "No, Annie, you will not live your life as a stone!"

The tears flowed. I sobbed and sobbed and sobbed and sobbed.

All the pain and suffering I had buried flowed out of me;

Thus began the beginning of the healing of my heart.

PART 3
THE THATCHED COTTAGE

The thatched cottage in the wilderness,

representing safety and warmth;

the lone candle aglow in the window,

all else darkness.

Oh, how this light would call me inside.

I knew if I could make it inside, I would be okay,

but I did not know how.

I stood outside in the darkness in the forest,

shaking and shivering with the cold,

longing more than anything to go inside to the warmth,

envisioning the feeling inside.

Time after time, the light called me; it never went out,

and yet I stood outside,

praying I would find my way inside the cottage.

Until one day, I finally made it inside.

I flung open the doors and windows to let the sunshine in;

unknown to me the cottage represented my heart.

The light in my heart had never left me,

the sunlight now representing the healing occurring in my life!

Annie Baatz

THE
STORY
OF
SURVIVAL

PART 1
MY MARRIAGE

My marriage was good for many years, and we had
two beautiful daughters who brought much joy
into our lives. Many beautiful memories that will
always be cherished.

The years passed, our daughters grew and life was
passing me by at a high speed, and things started to
change for me. I knew my marriage was over,
nothing was working any more. I was always
anxious and very tense.

Then I lost myself, so busy taking care of everyone else, I forgot
about me. The everyday humdrum of life, day after day,
Week after week, month after month, year after year.
I followed the existence of my life.
My body and Spirit became more and more weary.
I wore sadness like a blanket; it was such a part of who I was.
Trying to find beauty in my gardens, the laughter of my children.
But deep within, I was losing myself more and more.
I turned to alcohol. I had to escape the lonliness, the sadness.
It brought me comfort at the time, eased the anxiety, and enabled
me to sleep. I started to depend on it more and more. I could not
stand how I felt inside every day, and it became a huge part of my
life; it was my only escape from this world. I lost myself more
and more in this cycle of darkness.
I knew I wanted to leave, but the financial struggles were real.

I did not earn enough money to provide everything we would need.

Where would we live? How could I pay for all the necessities?

My car barely worked; I never knew if it would get me to work or not.

So I stayed, comforting myself with the sunrise and the sunset,

the beauty of my gardens;

then winter set in, and there was nothing for me to hang on to.

My despair and sadness growing deeper and deeper.

I was in therapy at the time. My therapist ran retreats over the world, and there was one in the process of happening; she suggested that I go. I was so desperate for anything that would help me feel better. I had never been on a retreat, and I asked her what it was about. I did not hear her response, but I took her suggestion and went. It was amazing; boulders, weights I had been carrying on my shoulders, fell off; I started to trust. These retreats were helping me to grow, to overcome whatever was going on in my life, and I had a lot going on.

Leaving the retreat and heading home, I knew in my heart

of hearts, it was over and it was time for me to leave.

I made the decision to leave. I packed my clothes.

I said to myself, "What are you doing, Annie? You have

nowhere to go,"

and a little voice inside me said, "Just take one more step, Annie."

It was one of the hardest things I ever had to do; I was scared of everything even my own shadow.

I filed for divorce; it was something I had only ever imagined, and now here I was in a lawyer's office filing the paperwork. I know God was with me as I had the courage of a spider.

I called a real estate agent to look at apartments in my area; I wanted to keep my daughters close by their friends.

As fate would have it,

an apartment fell into my lap and all of its belongings.

I took out a loan and purchased the contents of the home.

Friends gave me things;

within days it was painted, carpets cleaned, everything sparkling.

Friends came to help and encourage.

My Spirit started to become alive, feeling strong, yet the fear never left, I had no belief in my own self, starting out on my own.

At night, I called on the arch angels to comfort me:

Michael, Gabriel, and Raphael, who represent strength, courage, and healing;

and I called on Jesus Christ to sit on my bed to protect me.

Night after night, I sought comfort from my nightly companions who protected me during the darkness until sunlight found its waythrough the windows.

It has taken years of work in therapy to find my way. I am still on this journey of finding out who I am, and following the path towards freedom of myself and others. It has been a long journey, but now I am in a place where I have made peace within and with those around me.

However, I also now had to accept my part in my marriage. I had not been the best wife, mother, friend. The guilt I carried was intense. I was a victim for many years. There were times I was not proud of who I was, how I behaved, the person I had become, my thoughts and actions, the choices I had made. I had to make peace with my behavior if I wanted freedom from myself. It took years of work, and today my past actions do not haunt me. My past is in the past, and I move forward to try to be the best version of myself that I can be. Taking a good look at yourself takes a lot of courage, to dig deep inside exposing so much vulnerability, to realize how big the EGO really is, to accept responsibility, to make amends for my actions, to now do better, act better, live a better life is so freeing…

As a result of me having the courage to leave and find my way, everyone else has found happiness in their own lives, creating their own paths, and their own journey. We all have to create our own happiness, follow our own inner voice. There have been situations where we have come together as a family to support each other.

PART 2
THE STORM

Six weeks after moving into my new home,

News reports of Super Storm Sandy hitting the East Coast were broadcasted daily.

My daughters went to stay with friends. I decided to stay.

The bridges were closed, shutting off access; we were barricaded in.

I walked to the ocean; the powerful waves were already over the sand dunes.

I had never seen anything like this.

I walked home; my intuition told me to pack a small bag, a change of clothes for us,

Important documents and my mother's jewelry.

I moved my car to a high spot not knowing how I would get back home;

the water already covered the roadways.

As fate would have it, someone was swapping out a car that was parked right in front of me.

He saw me sitting in my car and offered me a ride home. A miracle.

The wind was fierce: the spray of the water hitting my face.

I had a quiet peacefulness inside, and I had no idea what was about to unfold.

Within a short time, the water started to come up through the floor in my home

and seep in under the door.

Ever so calmly, I unplugged every outlet; the power went out.

My small bag sitting by the couch.

Suddenly, my landlord appeared, opened the door, and the water gushed inside;

he took me upstairs to their home.

The water flowed violently down the street, quickly rising.

My landlord went to rescue an elderly lady next door, and we sat in the kitchen cold, scared, and so frightened.

Then the sound of crackling wood filled the air.

The houses started to catch fire; sparks the size of the palm of my hand filled the air.

The houses behind us and to the side of us were going up in flames.

There was no escape; the shed behind us caught fire.

I tried to devise a plan of escape; there was nowhere to go,

The water was still gushing at a high speed outside, and fires were everywhere.

I was not afraid. I looked up to heaven and said,

"God, if it is my time to go, thank you for making me the woman I am today, and tell my children I love them!"

I lay down in a bed and listened to the sound of the wood burning outside, knowing I had to rest.

Again, as FATE would have it, my landlord's son arrived on the only truck that made it into Rockaway during the storm; I can describe it as something from the Navy Seals. A small group of people in wet suits came into the house and got us. The water up over my waist, I carried my small bag over my head, and they loaded us on the truck. I could not believe what I was seeing: the fires, the flames, the water. I shook uncontrollably from the cold, from what I had just experienced. Two other families somehow got on this truck; I vaguely remember seeing people carrying children on their shoulders and getting on the truck.

As we crossed the bridge, I could not believe what I was seeing. Dozens of fire trucks, police cars, ambulances all lined up unable to venture across as the water level was too high. What was going to happen to all those homes on fire? They would burn down.

The cell towers were down; I was unable to contact my daughters. They put us on a school bus and took us to an old military base by the bridge. They were not prepared for us; it was cold, and they gave us old gray harsh blankets. I wrapped up my neighbor. They were able to charge their phones and get in touch with family who came for them. My landlord got in touch with his son, and his son came to get them. I tried to contact my daughters using his phone, but no response. My phone was dead, so I could not contact a friend as I did not know the numbers. When their son arrived, he said, "I am not taking them with us," meaning me and the elderly lady. I could not believe he was going to leave us there, leave us in this cold military base sitting in wet clothes; and I knew my landlord felt bad leaving us, but he had no other choice. How could a human being have no concern for another human being given what we had just experienced? They left us there. We finally ended up in a shelter, a gymnasium in a school, after much movement around. They gave us dry socks. My elderly neighbor did not want me to leave her side; she was so fearful. We got a cot in the gym, some blankets, and exhaustion overcame us. We were a sight for sore eyes. When I woke up, the gymnasium was filled with cots, families, children, infants; all was lost to so many.

My friend came to get me; my daughters were safe. I stayed in a hotel, thanks to my job. I could not believe life was normal; people going on with the business of life, and just a few miles away there was so much destruction, chaos, people's lives turned upside down, never to be the same again. I could not take my elderly neighbor with me, I told her to rest and I would come back for her. I brought her to the school office, and called her daughter. The lady in the office said she would take care of her. I did not want to leave her, but I had to get my car, and check on my daughters.

Then came the full awareness of the impact and devastation of the storm. I went to visit my home that I had just left six weeks prior, and there was 5 ft of water on the first floor. Windows were off the ledge; everything was in chaos, all entwined in sand and water. I could not believe the destruction. Houses were lifted on their foundations; decks were detached from their homes, lying on their sides and some a distance from their homes. Children's toys were scattered everywhere; it was hard to accept. Then to my new home, all destroyed, and my few belongings gone; everything had to be thrown out on the sidewalk. House after house, the piles of everyone's belongings took over the sidewalk. Friends came to help me clean out the apartment. A great friend took a few of my clothes that were hanging up and my daughters' christening clothes and first communion dresses to clean them. All else lost, and then the reality hit. Now what? Where do we live? What will happen to us? The apartment uninhabitable. I cried and cried and had to keep moving. My prior home had to be taken care of; it was left vacant after the storm. Day after day, I went to clean it out. Every day, I signed up at the Habitat for Humanity tables to try to get volunteers to help; hundreds came daily, but that was not enough. No house had escaped the destruction. Seven days of long hours and the help of volunteers. We had everything scraped down to the bare beams.

The pain and suffering I seen on my daughters' faces when they realized everything they had was gone was so painful; their expressions of disbelief will stay with me to the day I die. They had the clothes they wore the day they left to stay with friends and whatever few things they packed.

Life continued in the outside world, and I stayed with friends who opened their homes to me. My daughters stayed with their friends, and I got to see them every day I visited to clean out the homes. I did not know how we would find a new place to live as the entire area was evacuated. No power. People just came to take care of their home during sunlight, and as dusk set at 4:30 p.m., the line of cars to exit the peninsula was miles long.

After the exhaustive work of taking care of what needed to be done, my brain stopped working. I could not function properly. I could only focus on the task at hand. When that was done, I could only focus on the next thing; I could not look at the whole day. It was too overwhelming for me.

In the midst of this crisis came the gas shortage. Day after day, people waited three to four hours to get gas. Police presence at every gas station was necessary as people were on edge. One night after cleaning my home, I had to get gas. My main priority was seeing my children. I waited in line one night for three hours to get gas, freezing cold as I could not turn on the heat and lose what little gas I had. I was so dirty after hours of throwing things out, and I just wanted a shower. My old car broke down; the cars behind me moved ahead of me. I begged for someone to jump my car; no one had cables. Everyone wanted to make sure they got gas before it shut down at the curfew of midnight. I was only one block from the gas station. I got out of my car and walked to the gas station. The power was out, and there were no streetlights. I begged a gentleman to please help me; he was pumping gas into the little red containers to have extra. I looked like a beggar. He did not want to help me. I told him I had just lost everything in the storm; I needed to be able to see my daughters. I was so distraught. He finally showed mercy toward me and told me to get into his car. We drove around and I could not find my car. It was dark. He thought I was lying to him that my car broke down. I told him I was not. We drove around again, and I spotted my car in behind the line of cars. He jumped my car, but it would not start. I started to panic. What would happen to me? I had no phone service. I could not contact the hotel to get me, and it was dark. He tried three times to start my car, and then he said we would try one more thing. He told me exactly what to do, and I followed his direction. My engine started. I got out of my car and threw my arms around him in gratitude, told him he was my angel, got back in line for gas, and made it to the gas station in time. I filled up my car, and the gas station closed right after that. Another miracle.

I had to hire a truck to move some things from my previous home upstairs for fear of looters. It was very difficult to hire a truck as there was no gas to fill them. I finally got a truck with under a tank of gas. The only storage facility available was almost an hour away. There was nothing available. My good friend located it for me. It was not an easy task at all to move the furniture and few things into the truck.

My friend arranged to meet me at the storage facility, and with the help of her cousins, we moved some belongings to safety. Now I had to return the truck. The gas tank was almost on empty. I got lost. I was way out of my way. Here I was driving a truck around Queens and Brooklyn with no idea where I was going. My GPS got me lost. I was panicking, and I was fearful of running out of gas. Then what? I pulled into a gas station; there was no gas to be had, and I stopped a man walking into the store area. I was at the end of my rope. All this stress was just too much for me; my brain was barely working at that time. He pointed out which way to go, and I told him what had happened to me, and that I was almost out of gas and there was no room for error. This man went out of his way for miles and miles and directed me to go straight and that I would reach my destination. I thanked him, threw my arms around him in gratitude, and he said, "God bless you." Again another miracle. I made it to the truck return, the gas level below empty.

A few short months later, sitting at my friend's kitchen table, discussing how to find a new place to live and get my life back in motion, my friends offered me the opportunity for a new home. I was so delighted to have somewhere to move into. Friends got together and threw me a shower of all the necessities I would need to start again. Someone gave me a bed; the kindness of people made it possible for me to have what I needed to live a daily life. Another miracle.

I kept asking, "How could this happen?" It took all the courage I had to leave my marriage, my home, move into an apartment, and lose everything again. Why?

Trying to pick up the pieces and function as a normal human being was not easy. With the help of good friends, an amazing therapist, and the unconditional support of my family, I started finding my feet again.

As I look back on these times, there were many blessings, and I can see a lot of it happened for my own good and that of my children!

PART 3
THE INVASION

A few months later, after settling into our new home,

the invasion of unwanted visitors came into our home in the form of bed bugs.

These creatures disrupted our lives, mentally and physically.

I was barely finding my feet, and now the lack of sleep caused by this invasion put me in a darker place than where I was already.

They invaded my living room; my new couch was infested.

I screamed when I saw what seemed to be hundreds of them.

I could not believe what I was seeing. These insects were hidden in the seams of the couch, the cushions.

Oh my God. What was happening to me?

I immediately called some friends about what to do. I had heard of bed bugs and the devastation they caused in people's lives, but I never imagined they could invade my home.

My friend told me to throw the couch out. We just had the couch a few months, and my daughter and I lifted the couch outside. I was afraid they would get on my clothes. I was told to call an exterminator, and I did. It was late at night when this was happening. I checked the bedrooms and did not see anything there. Needless to say, I did not sleep that night envisioning these creatures crawling over me.

The exterminator arrived the next morning with a list of directions for me. I was so overwhelmed and distraught that he had to keep repeating himself. He sprayed everywhere and found some of these bedbugs in the bedrooms. These were not just regular bugs. These bugs sucked your blood to grow. That was how they lived. OMG, how could this be? I was in shock. I had bug bites on my body. Just the thought of bugs being in my bed overwhelmed me, and the idea of them crawling all over me and drinking my blood was too much for me to comprehend. Everything had to be washed in hot water and dried on high heat, bagged, and left in the basement of a good friend, who was kind enough to help us. The exterminator came three times to follow up and advised me to keep checking as they laid eggs. The list of things to do was like climbing a mountain, to go through each book page by page, go through each shoe as they got into everything. They invaded my personal space without my permission, in my own home, and there was not much I could do to control them. We had to go through the process. The work was a nightmare. Finally, I could not take much more. I threw out so much stuff. It was just too much, and I could not sleep at night. I could not go to work. My brain did not function correctly. This whole process lasted seven weeks until my home was clear. I went to the doctor's office one day. I did not know what else to do. She wanted to put me on anti-anxiety medication, and I said no. I just wanted someone to listen to me. Even though my home was clear, my mind could not rest. I was not able to rest or sleep for many months after that, always wondering if they were crawling over my body. It was December, and we put up a tree. There was not much of a Christmas spirit in our home that year. So much had happened in such a short time.

Night after night of no sleep took its toll on me. The disbelief again, my home invaded this time by bugs.

What little we had had to be thrown out. I was still trying to find my feet after losing everything in Super Storm Sandy. The hardest part was seeing my daughter's face in disbelief, taking her clothes out of the dryer, and seeing they were destroyed. She did not have much to begin with, and now she had even less. She asked me, "Why is this happening to me?" I could not answer her. The pain was written all over her face.

A few weeks later, I thought everything was clear. I was sitting in my bed saying my prayers, and I felt something on my shoulder. I turned around, and there was a bed bug on my pillow. I jumped out of my bed, got on my two knees, and begged God to help me. I thought I was going insane; I could not go through this again. The exterminator did not want to come back, and I begged. He sent someone, a woman, and she had so much compassion for me. The bedbugs had laid eggs. A home is the place we go to escape the outside world, and when your home is invaded by bedbugs, there is no escape from anything anywhere. I cried so much in therapy. I wanted my therapist to tell me I was going to be okay, and she could not. At this stage, I did not know if I was going to be okay. My nerves were stretched as far as they could go. I was at the end of my rope. I could not take any more pain, suffering and loss.

I was in disbelief. All I could say was, "Again? Again?

Lose everything again? How can this be?"

I left my house with my basic items.

Left everything behind me.

Got a new apartment, lost everything to the invasion of water.

Got another new home, lost everything to unwanted creatures.

All within 16 months.

To lose everything, even my own blood, was beyond comprehension.

I became so angry with God. I kicked and screamed.

I was beyond traumatized at this point.

My brain was not functioning very well;

all I could do was cry and cry and cry.

Financial struggles were very real. How would we survive?

I was taking loan after loan to get by.

The darkness I was in got very dark.

I wanted to die; I was more than exhausted.

My body was mentally, physically, and spiritually bankrupt.

The desire to go on was no longer there.

The will to die was so strong, but God said, "No, it's not your time."

I screamed constantly at God at how my life had unfolded.

I did not want to communicate with him,

yet that part of me could still see the light on the ocean,

the moon and the stars, the beauty in the clouds.

Today, I know I was carried through those times like the poem

"Footsteps in the Sand."

I was unable to carry myself. I was beyond, beyond wanting to stay in this physical world.

I wanted to escape.

PART 4
THE COURTS

The lawyers, the courts, and the judges became a part of my journey.

Through all my trials and traumatic experiences, I had to show up for life.

The unfeeling judge.

The trauma of standing on the trial stand.

My husband's lawyer had no compassion.

Question after question, accusation after accusation.

My insides were shaking.

I had no idea which angle she was going to come from.

At least 90 minutes on the stand, she tried to prove me to be someone I was not.

She traumatized me from the inside out;

my whole body was shaking.

It was like something I would watch on TV.

The court's verbiage

lasting six years.

My life on hold

at the mercy of everyone else.

I was just another person walking through the revolving doors of justice.

Everyone unaware of the traumas that were unfolding in my life.

At the mercy of the NY court system.

Month after month.

Year after year.

Situations arising that did not seem real,

yet they were. Postponement after postponement.

Then the worst thing that could possibly could have happened happened to me;

my lawyer dropped me.

I questioned her on something. She did not like it,

and I never heard from her for months on end.

Not only was my case stressful and my life on hold,

but now I had no communication with my lawyer.

I could not understand what was happening.

Again, I trusted, and again, I was dropped like a hot potato.

I called and called, left messages, and nothing. No communication.

They always got back to me when I had a question. Now only silence.

What would happen to me? How could this happen again?

It was hard for me to trust, and I trusted her.

And the trust was broken again.

Now what? Where did I go from here?

Hiring a new lawyer was starting the process all over again;

no one wanted to take on someone else's case.

I had to accept what happened, keep praying, and keep surrendering.

I just thought to myself that something has to happen at some stage.

One day, approximately six months later, I received a phone call from my lawyer

Stating she wanted to see me. I could not believe what was happening. I waited a few days

to respond as I was so hurt and so angry with her. How could she just drop me like that?

How could she do that to another human being after everything we had been through?

I went to see her, and she acted as if nothing had happened. I let her know I was upset with her and

how she treated me.

We had to go back to court, back in the system again, all these years later.

Still no closure. Now a new judge, more compassion, still moving through the

NY court system.

I wanted closure on that part of my life,

to be able to pick up the pieces and move forward as best as I could through this life;

but for now, I had to keep surrendering.

THE DARKNESS
THE TRAP DOORS

Sadness occupied every fiber of my being.

I had lost myself.

I fumbled around unsure of what was happening to me.

My marriage over.

My FEAR to leave unbearable.

Find a new place to live; six weeks later lose it all in the storm.

Another trap door opened, and I fell.

The trauma of what had occurred,

the pain, the suffering.

Where do I go? What do I do? The financial struggles real.

Feeling ever so powerless and helpless;

the look of sadness in my daughters' eyes was too much for me to bear.

All was lost to them; their belongings destroyed.

What now?

New home, another invasion. This time unwanted visitors

Put me over the edge,

And I fell through another door.

The lawyers, the courts , the judges.

The darkness, the loneliness, the despair, the sadness.

The trap doors continued to open, and it got darker and darker.

I trudged through daily life barely alive inside.

My Spirit was dying more and more.

My light was going out.

I could not go on nor did I want to.

The rollercoaster ride I was on was too much for me to handle.

I cried oceans of tears; the sadness and darkness settled over me,

And I kept falling through the trap doors.

I was tumbling into the darkness at a fast speed.

I did not have the energy to try to climb out anymore.

Darkness became my existence; I lived there for years.

Dying more and more on the inside.

Gone beyond the help of human aid.

I was so far gone, no human could help me.

SADNESS

Woah!!!! Sadness, darkness.

It comes so quietly.

Descending upon me, unseen, entering through the back door,

yet I see it.

Like the morning dew settles on the grass blades,

the sadness settles over my being.

And with it brings tears

and brings me to a place I don't want to go; touches the depths of my soul I did not know could even

exist.

The part I wish to let go.

Part of me is fighting,

fighting for my life.

The boxing ring.

Yet many times, the sadness wins.

The tears I have cried, the pain and the suffering. Oh, the suffering.

I pray for God's grace to release me,

to let me have the freedom I am so fighting for.

I long for the light, the light of hope to stay lit

like the glow of light in a lone thatched cottage window,

welcoming me into safety.

I see the glow so inviting;

I yearn to go inside.

Yes, to go in, and leave the sadness outside.

I go step by step forward in this life;

sometimes backwards, falling many times,

yet God always gives me the strength and courage to get back up.

I hope one day God's grace and mercy will bestow upon me a gift.

A gift of light,

a light to the world

to keep going,

keep fighting till the end,

to release me from this bondage to freedom!

THE TURNING POINT

I remember so clearly,

the darkness so real.

I pulled my car over by the ocean.

I screamed at God, "I can't take anymore!"

I do not know what occurred in that moment,

but in my heart, I know God said,

"Yes, Annie. It's enough. It's enough."

Thus began my journey back to the land of the living.

It was a long road.

I had lived in the dark for so many years.

I did not know how to exist back in the land of the living.

I was like an infant learning to walk.

I had to take a step at a time on wobbly feet;

I stumbled many times.

It was a difficult journey to be in a world where everything seemed normal,

And I had to learn to be a part of it again as a functioning human being.

I know in that moment in the car, God graced me with His mercy and has carried me many times.

The dark that had consumed me for so long was no longer so scary.

I had to learn to be in the light,

to learn new things;

but in the darkness, I have gained much wisdom.

So much awareness that no one can take from me.

These are inside gifts.

They are my treasures,

the gifts from God through my struggles.

He never let me go!

LONGING

When will I be enough for me?

When will I surrender to Him who knows best?

When can I walk into a room, anytime, anywhere, and know I am enough?

When can I look in the mirror and say, "You are enough, Annie. You are enough."

I think of that time. I long for that time

Where I can connect with my authentic being,

The being of authenticity, of love, of beauty.

No dark shadows, only light.

Carefree of the thoughts of the world.

To connect with my inner light

Brings me much joy, much love, much comfort, much peace.

One day, step by step, I walk this path to me to God,

my guardian, my Spirit guide, my hidden treasure!

JOURNEY TO SELF-LOVE

How does one love one's self?

I had never thought about it;

I was never aware of that.

I loved others, never myself.

In the darkness, I learned about me, how to care for me.

My heart had been broken;

for a time, there was no love,

only emptiness and sadness.

I longed for love, to give it, and receive it.

I did not know how to do that.

I was watching Super Soul Sunday with Oprah Winfrey.

She said she had interviewed someone; I cannot remember who.

This person had a hard time with love,

so she said she wrote on a piece of paper, "I love you. I really love you"

and put it on her bathroom mirror, so she would see it every day.

She did this for 30 days, but then continued it until one day she believed it.

Oprah said, "Well, if she can do it, so can I!"

I said, "If Oprah Winfrey can try this, then so can I."

I wrote "I love you, Annie. I really love you" on a piece of blue paper

Very small, and I put it in the bottom corner of my bathroom mirror,

as I did not believe it, and I did not want it glaring in front of me.

Yet this small piece of blue paper caught my attention every time,

And I said it over and over and over until one day I really meant it.

I practiced with people I would meet.

In my mind, I would say, "with love."

For months and months, I practiced love,

Love for me and love for others.

I learned self-care, to take care of me, to use my voice, to set boundaries.

Being kind to myself,

saying "No" as a full sentence,

prayer and meditation.

Lo and behold, one day I looked in the mirror and from the depths of my being,

I looked at the woman in the mirror, and I knew I had learned to love me.

What a gift I have received, the priceless and most treasured gift of all. Love.

Love for myself and love for others.

What a journey I am on.

Thank you, God, for the dark,

for without it, I would never have discovered the greatest gift ever!

"Love"

THE WARRIOR SELF

My warrior self,

She visits me in my dreams.

She is always there,

Ready to serve and protect me.

She is dressed as a Viking at sea.

Her sword sharp.

She stands steadfast,

Ready to protect a precious gift locked behind an iron gate.

So strong and confident in herself,

She knows she can beat an army.

That precious gift, my vulnerability.

Through my journey, my vulnerability was exposed.

She could not be contained until the warrior came.

She comes to protect us, to keep us safe.

I stand in awe of how brave and strong she is;

The comfort in knowing she is a part of me.

I call on her when I need her.

She is always there and takes over,

Relieving me of indecision.

Another gift in my life, my Warrior Princess!

A PRAYER FOR ME
MY HOPES AND DREAMS

I pray for peace, love, and hope in my life,

that I continue on this journey toward the light, to God.

To trust God more and more,

to have more faith and wisdom,

to face all challenges that come my way

knowing that these lessons are for me

to take another step on the path to liberation.

I pray for strength and courage,

for more insights,

to pay attention to my intuition.

To stand strong when the storms come crashing

and not be like the leaf,

blown here and there.

I pray for health, so I can continue the dojo.

So I can get stronger and stronger

to be available for my daughters

mentally, physically, and spiritually for many years to come.

I pray for friends in my life, good friends, who believe in me and support me.

I pray my daughters will continue their path of growth and health,

that our relationships grow healthier and healthier.

I pray my family and friends stay close.

I pray to keep my five senses,

so I can continue to watch the sunrise and sunset

and always maintain my connection with nature.

I pray for my dreams, my home on the ocean, my retreat home in nature.

That I always be guided by the forces

to step into the woman God has intended me to be.

I pray to help people in the world

and to have compassion and forgiveness for them all!

BELONGING

My heart yearns to be accepted,

to be fully embraced by me, all of me.

I see me wanting to embrace me, to love me, to honor me.

I see the ocean, the waves; my connection is so beautiful

to the breeze, to the beauty, the wonder, the power, the strength.

I feel God's nudge

reminding me He is always there;

to Him I belong.

That is all that really matters in this world.

All other sense of belonging is but a flight

quickly passing,

but my belonging to the source, to the power,

is a gift I am slowly allowing myself to receive!

MY JOURNEY OF THE SELVES

Selves, oh so many selves.

Discovering each other.

What a joy.

A revelation of being,

the God self, the inner child, the warrior, the inner critic,

the strong, the courageous, the weak, the fearful,

yet we are one.

The journey of finding each other

like long-lost friends,

the meeting of each other,

the merging of our souls,

knowing if we bring down the walls

we find such happiness

in discovering and sharing each other's story.

Knowing we will merge one day,

as equals into one being,

and with God's grace

find the hidden gems in life,

enjoy to the last second,

this beautiful world we live in

knowing we have made a difference in people's lives!

NATURE

The embracing leaves

so soft and tender,

blowing so gently

soothing my soul.

The breeze so full of energy

Wrapping me in a cocoon of love.

The clouds

all so different,

reminding me of the stages of my life.

Big and beautiful.

Dark and dreary.

The sun peeking through with hope.

The chimes of love,

the aroma of nature,

the birds chirping,

the magic of it all;

where I can close my eyes

and get swept away to my own being.

THE TENDER MOMENT

The Sufi music

bringing me to a place of freedom

like a ballerina in the sky,

soaring up and up to freedom,

touching the depths of my being.

Soaring, soaring, twirling, twirling.

Wrapped in rainbow colors by something not seen,

finally diving

through the head to the heart.

THE CLOUDS

The clouds.
I travel through these clouds
not sure where I am going,
blinded by the unknown.
Trying to find my way.
The darkness.
The light,
The turbulence,
Yet the light peeks through
giving me hope,
reaching my soul to the very depths;
the comfort I feel makes me want to cry.
So I keep moving forward,
trusting where I am going
is where I am meant to be.
Never finding a destination,
but trusting the light to guide me!

FORGIVENESS
FORGIVENESS OF SELF AND OTHERS

How does one forgive one's self, and more importantly, how does one forgive those who have caused him or her so much pain and suffering?

My pain was deep.

My suffering unbearable.

The anger, the resentment, the guilt

That I carried for others and myself in my heart consumed me.

I carried these heavy boulders on my back everywhere I went.

The weight was tremendous,

but I was not willing to part with these emotions

until one day, they became unbearable.

I listened to the voices of my elders

Suggesting if I wanted freedom

I would have to pray for them everything I wanted for myself, and I wanted

peace, love, good friends, serenity, kindness, forgiveness, compassion.

My defiant self said, "no"; my Spirit self said, "yes."

Night after night, I prayed on my knees for those who had hurt me,

Not meaning one word I said but wanting freedom for myself.

I prayed through gritted teeth.

Sometimes all I could say was "You know what I mean."

My pain was so great. I continued this journey for years

Until one night, I realized I actually meant what I said.

I really wanted them to have all the gifts I wanted for myself,

And in that moment, I was set free.

The boulders I had been carrying fell from my shoulders,

And the greatest blessing of all is that I was free and that I

Was the one who received all the gifts, love, peace,

Compassion, forgiveness, kindness, serenity.

What a gift!

COMPASSION

What is compassion?

Compassion to me brings empathy
For the sorrows of the world,
a world so confused,
the beliefs so incorrect,
the wars, the deaths, the loss of life for what?
The world has lost what is important: family, friends, care and love
for one another,
truth, honesty, and faith.

War after war,
death after death,
life after life fighting for causes,
which are not worth fighting for.

WHAT IS KINDNESS?

Kindness is when your life turns upside down, and the Universe responds!

Kindness is when you have nowhere to go, and people open their homes to you.

Kindness is when you have no food, and someone takes you into their kitchen and says, "Take what you want."

Kindness is when someone says to you, "What do you need?"

Kindness is when someone gives you a hug in the midst of despair.

Kindness is when someone restarts your car after waiting in line for three hours to get gas and does not give up until it starts.

Kindness is when someone goes out of their way for miles to put you in the right direction when you are lost.

Kindness is when great friends offer you a home to move into.

Kindness is when someone shows up to your home with a bed.

Kindness is when people get together and give you a shower to have the necessities to start again.

Kindness is when someone gives you hats and gloves when you don't have any.

Kindness is when a special friend opened her home in nature to me so I could escape the realities of life for a few days.

Kindness is when a great friend offered me a place to come and workout.

Kindness is the smile that touches my heart.

Kindness is when someone sat beside me and held my hand and did not say anything.

Kindness of the Universe

sweeping me up,

putting people in my path to help me.

Ensuring I stay connected to the ocean and the stars,

sending angels from Heaven,

to guide and encourage me to put one foot in front of each other,

to take care of me when my mind was so traumatized.

God never left me through this darkness.

Through the kindness of God,

I know what is important in my life today.

Material existence can be wiped out in a second,

But spiritual existence is truth!

No one can ever take this from me.

The relationship that I have with my Higher Power today

Is the most important thing in my life.

He is the light that I see in the flowers, the trees,

The ocean,

Always reminding me He is there.

I am wealthy in Spirit,

And every step of my journey brought me to now!

HOPE ON THE MATS

I punch the bag for the pain and suffering of the loss of my once best friend.

I punch the bag for Super Storm Sandy and everything that came with it.

I punch the bag for all the years of darkness and hopelessness.

I punch the bag for the loss of so many years.

I punch the bag for the pain and suffering my daughters have endured.

I punch the bag for the emptiness and loneliness and the feeling of being so lost.

I punch the bag for the anger I have felt.

I punch the bag for the lawyers, the courts, the judges, for the powerlessness over my divorce.

I punch the bag for the hopes and dreams of my beautiful daughters.

Today, I punch the bag for my life.

I punch the bag to fight my way back to the land of the living.

I punch the bag for hope, for a beautiful life for me and my daughters.

I punch the bag to fight for my body, for strength and courage,

to keep going in this life especially when I don't want to.

I punch the bag to a new freedom of love

and friends and hopes and dreams.

The light that I follow in my heart

to pave the way for those coming behind me,

who in darkness have lost all hope.

I fight for people all over the world

that they too find freedom inside.

Today, I bow to Professor Vee, whom I know I would have loved
and cherished and for everything he represented.
I bow to Professor David,
Whom without his kindness and determination,
I would not have the bag to fight for my life
And that of humanity.

WHAT IS LOVE TO ME TODAY?

Love is the gentle breeze that touches my skin when the air is still.

Love is the wave of the leaves briskly blowing when the forest is quiet.

Love is when my heart misses a beat when the sun starts to rise.

Love is seeing the beauty of the stars, knowing we are connected.

Love is the light in my heart always waiting patiently for me to return home.

Love is when my dog looks in my eyes seeing the very depths of my being.

Love is being touched by grace.

Love is being compassionate with myself.

Love is knowing everything happens for my own good.

Love is when my heart and mind connect.

Human love always changes.

Divine love never changes;

Divine love is truth!

LETTER TO GOD

Dear God,

Thank you for being my guiding light.

Thank you for the waves, the dark, thundering, overpowering waves.

I had to sink and fall to the bottom,

So I could learn to swim.

Thank you for the sunrise and sunset;

they show me your power, your love, and your beauty.

Thank you for the stars that remind me you are there,

always giving me hope.

Thank you for the nudges in my heart

that remind me you are always there.

I am your daughter.

Guide me in my life's path

to be like you,

to get to know you better,

to trust you more and more with my life.

Above all, I look forward to the day we meet.

I know our connection is strong;

with each situation, the bond grows stronger.

Surrender. Surrender. Surrender.

I love you now and always,

Annie

A LETTER FROM MY INNER CHILD TO ME

Dear Annie,

You still forget I exist

In your busy life.

I love it when you remember me.

It makes me feel special.

I am a child

who has to know she is loved.

I am so proud of you

and how far you have come.

I lived a very sad life before you knew I existed.

Very lonely, always vulnerable.

I was so excited when you heard I existed

and when you paid attention to me.

I am always going to be with you,

so please remember to check in with me

especially when you are going through things;

that is when I need comfort the most.

I love being with you.

I love to see you grow and take care of you.

I am so grateful to you, your inner child.

Love always, your baby Joy.

A LETTER FROM ME TO MY INNER CHILD, JOY

Dear Joy,

I am also so excited to know you exist.

You are a very important part of my life.

I am really sorry I did not know you existed;

you were so alone,

so vulnerable for most of my life.

I will try harder to remember you are with me,

A part of me,

to connect with you regularly.

I love you so much.

I can see you like an angel,

so very beautiful.

I am grateful for you too,

And will always love you.

You now hold a very special place in my heart.

I look forward to our journey together.

To love, to grow, to cry, to dance, to sing.

Loving you and sending a big hug.

Your guardian,

Annie

MY SOUL

What is my soul?

My Spirit knows deep within me,

the connection to the moon and the stars,

the sunrise, the sunset, the ocean, the light.

I see the light around me

In the leaves, the grass, the flowers,

the children.

To experience moments of not being in this human body;

to know there is something more to this life than what I am living,

something in the Spiritual realm,

the unseen.

My journey now is to follow my heart,

to be the Captain of my Soul,

to fulfill my dreams,

to make a difference in the world,

to bring light where there is darkness,

to bring hope to the hopeless,

to bring joy where there is sadness,

to encourage others to follow their passions, their dreams.

To be a beacon of light, of courage, of strength from my little corner of the world,

to leave this world a better place,

to have touched a life,

to bring a smile.

This is the journey of my soul.

That my experiences may help others,

to follow my intuition, my dreams,

knowing I am on my way home!

That is where I long to be,

Away from the struggles,

away from this life

to be one with my Creator.

Away from the sadness of this world,

the sadness I see in people's eyes;

the suffering throughout the world

is too much for this weary soul to handle.

The grief overwhelms me.

I need to go home to rest.

SURRENDER

Surrender is giving up control of my life

and how I think it should be.

Surrender is giving up the I, me, and mine.

Surrender to me requires faith and trust.

Trusting my Higher Power that whatever happens in my life is for my own good.

Faith is the absence of doubt.

Faith is taking the next step not knowing how things will unfold

but knowing everything will work out,

especially when it is for my higher good.

Suffering every day.

All situations that are presented to me bring freedom.

Being in this human body,

walking in this life,

I can only do mini surrenders.

Surrender egocentric desires,

so I can walk the spiritual path of love,

God's will for me, and what He wants.

Surrender is a conscious journey.

We are presented with many events

making us realize the need for surrender.

THE MISSING LINK

You are what I have been searching for.

You, who will make me complete.

My heart, my soul, my being

yearn to merge with you as one;

like a puzzle,

the final pieces make it complete.

I can see you through the waters,

you, me, who are one, representing beauty,

inner beauty, and light,

power and strength,

courage beyond courage,

compassion so great.

You see me as I truly am;

your heart represents safety,

a place of healing, of love, no judgment, unconditional love.

I see our fingers merge through the waters;

our hands connect as one,

yet I stand on the other side.

Alone and lost,

yearning for you

as you yearn for me.

You are so close and yet so far.

I pray one day we merge as one, as you

are the missing link to make my life complete.

RELATIONSHIP WITH MY HIGHER POWER

I was so confused.

My beliefs as a child regarding religion scared me.

"If you sin, you will go to hell.

If you are good, you go to heaven."

I stayed with this religion throughout my adult life

Until my mother passed away unexpectedly at a young age.

I had prayed to God to let her get better;

the doctors could not find out what was wrong

until it was too late. Cancer overtook her body.

I could not believe how this could happen.

I prayed and prayed for her to get better,

and she never made it home from the hospital.

The anger toward God was real.

I turned my back on church.

I screamed at God,

my pain and grief unbearable.

Unable to accept this loss,

the dark consumed me,

the sadness surrounded me;

I was unable to participate in life,

and my anger at God grew stronger.

As my journey continued,

and many traumas unfolded before me,

the darkness was everywhere.

I had to find something to hold on to.

I prayed to my mother.

I begged her to help me.

As the dark became darker,

I feared for my life.

I prayed to the ocean, to the moon, to the sun, and to the stars.

I needed something I could see.

My inner life was in turmoil,

And the weight of life became too much for me.

I would beg the moon and the stars to help me.

Somewhere deep inside, they are familiar to me.

I knew we had an inner connection that was beyond

what my human mind could comprehend.

I would beg them,

"Please don't forget me here."

"Please don't leave me here."

I wanted to go with them; they were familiar to my Spirit.

I would scream at the ocean in anger at how my life was unfolding;

my suffering was so deep, I wanted to die.

Yet that part of me stayed connected to that power I could see.

The power and beauty of the ocean,

the moon, the stars, the sunrise;

and I got to see there is something greater than me out there,

something that can create such beauty.

And that relationship started to grow

like a human relationship; it took work on my part.

Sometimes I was so angry and screamed,

and a few days later I would apologize.

I had to believe in this; I could see the beauty with human eyes.

Slowly, I began to see the beauty in the leaves, the flowers.

Hear the birds chirping; being present to the moment,

I grew internally.

I knew I needed more, someone to guide me.

Someone I could trust,

Someone to turn to.

And I prayed and prayed for this.

He came in the form of a Perfect Master,

Avatar Meher Baba from India.

Today, I know I am being guided.

I know everything happens for my own good

Even though I may not like it.

I know I am on a journey home.

But now I know I am never alone on this path.

What a blessing!

THE GIFTS

My journey,

The dark,

the tribulations,

the struggles

have presented me with many unexpected gifts.

The gift of awareness, to see what is happening in my life.

Gift of hope to keep moving forward in this life.

Gift of connection with the unseen.

Gift of desperation to take control of my life and to have the courage to create the life I want to live.

Gift of courage to take steps in my life I could only dream about.

Gift of love to have a heart full of love, for myself, and for those who hurt me.

Gift of faith to believe everything works out better than anything I could imagine.

Gift of living in the present moment to hear the birds. The sound of the ocean, the waves crashing down to get my attention to deliver its message. The sound of children laughing, to see the light in the leaves, the waves.

Gift of my intuition to pay attention to the messages it gives me.

Gift of peace appreciating the moments of peace and contentment even when life is happening around me.

Gifts of self-care to take care of me, setting boundaries, self-love, being kind and gentle with myself

Gifts of gratitude to be grateful for everything, for my struggles, the dark. To have peace in my home, to have food to eat, to have a bed to sleep in, to have money to pay my bills, for my job that gives me a paycheck, to have a lovely home by the ocean, to have great friends and family who love me; and I love them.

Gift of knowing I am here on this earth to find my purpose, to fulfill my dreams.

Gift of willingness to keep trying my best and not give up even if I want to.

Gift of my beautiful strong daughters encouraging and supporting me through this journey.

The greatest gift of all is with my Higher Power. I know today that whatever happens, I will be okay; that everything that has happened and will happen will be for the benefit of my soul on this journey through life, for my soul to evolve. That I am on the journey home, home to my true self, my higher self, to that which I long for, that connection beyond human understanding. That connection from which I came and to that which I shall return!

MY SPIRIT TODAY

Who are you?

I am the light you see in the ocean.

I am the light you see in the dark clouds.

I am the light you see in the leaves, the flowers, the grass.

I am the sound of chimes reminding you of peace and love.

I am the light you cry out to from the depths of your being.

I am the one you call to in sadness.

I am the light in the cottage window.

Your journey has been difficult,

Full of many obstacles and sadness.

I am the one who has kept the tiny glimmer of hope alive

When the rest of you wanted to die.

I am the One.

Even if you forget me,

I will always keep the light alive in you.

I am the one you talk to at night when you talk to the moon and the stars.

I am the light you look for at night outside your window,

Making sure you are being protected.

I am the one you connect with in the beauty of the sunrise,

The light glistening on the waves.

I will never leave you.

I just am!

WHERE DO I GO FROM HERE?
A NEW CHAPTER FOR THE REST OF MY LIFE!

Today, I am taking control of my life, to live the life I am meant to live. I will no longer allow my Spirit to be partially alive; I am meant to live a life of fullness, to step into the person I was created to be, to make my hopes and dreams a reality and not have them out there out of my reach. It is time for me to step into my courageous self.

I have joined an entrepreneur business called Kyani, a Health and Wellness company, which currently is registered in 64 countries worldwide. This is another stepping stone to become my authentic being. This is a gift that has been put into my life, and motivating me to overcome challenges . I know now it is not about me; it is about helping others find their way to create their own lives and visions. Through this program, I am now involved in a program called Caring Hands, and it is about helping people who are struggling to get food, schooling, and shelter. I have had my struggles with some of these, and I know I am on the right path.

Thanks to listening to the "Paradigm Shift" 2018 by Bob Proctor and Sandy Gallagher, I have made many decisions.

Bob said over and over "What do you want? What do you really want?" I felt I was the only person on this planet and that he spoke directly to my soul. He really made me think, what do I really want? I realized I want learn this material that is taught by the Proctor Gallagher Institute, to have time and financial freedom, and to teach it to others. I am now a consultant with the Thinking Into Results Program with the Proctor Gallagher Institute. This material speaks to me, and gives many tools to create a life of my dreams and inspire others.

Peggy McColl spoke on the "Paradigm Shift" and talked about the Book Author Program and that we all have a book inside us, and our story needs to be heard. I said, "I have a very good story to tell." Bob said, "If an intuitive thought comes, act on it, and don't think." I made the decision to write a book, sent an email to Peggy McColl, and the doors opened. Next thing I know I am enrolled in her Book Author Program. This is exactly how this book happened. I had no intention of writing a book; I did not ever think I could write a book, yet here I am. Yet again, I know it is not about me.

I am new to this world of changing my thinking, but I knew deep inside there is more to this world, this life than what I am living. I started to pay attention to different speakers but was so over-whelmed. I prayed for someone to be put in my path to guide me in this, and Bob Proctor appeared about 18 months ago.

Today, I am in awe. My Spirit is alive, and I am truly excited to watch my life unfold. To create my dreams, to hope this book touches someone's life, to never give up, to listen to that little voice inside that says take one more step, to know your struggles will bring you to a better place, the darkness will bring you into the light to a freedom that cannot be without the dark, to be okay when darkness comes, knowing it is for your higher good, to have hope for your future and believe if this fearful person can do this, then so can you.

Much love and light,

Annie

ABOUT THE AUTHOR

My name is Annie Baatz, and I was born in Co. Monaghan, Ireland and am one of seven children. Growing up with traditional Catholic religion, there was always Mass, say of the rosary in our home, baptism, communion and Confirmation.

I came to America in 1990, and got married, and have two beautiful daughters. The real journey of suffering started with losing my mother unexpectedly to cancer. She died at a young 58 years old in 2003. The inner turmoil started then, and has continued for many years to follow.

The journey of my life since then has been very turbulent, and much darkness took over my life; these were major traumatic events, over which I did not have any control. Today, after years of searching and praying, I am finding my way in this life, making many big decisions to live a life I am meant to live, for my Spirit to feel alive. I have a Higher Power in my life today, Avatar Meher Baba, which means Compassionate Father, a Perfect Master from India.

My hope today is to inspire people to never give up on life, to look for something to hang on to when life presents many challenges, to be a light for people to follow, to know if I can survive what I survived, and find my way, anyone can do it. I had no intention of writing this book, yet here it is. It was meant to be written, and I hope it touches people's lives all over the world. I am trusting the process of this book; I was told when something happens unexpectedly, it is a Gift from God. This book was unexpected, and so I now consider it a gift from me to the world.

It is my intention today and my purpose to find my way in this world, to allow my Spirit to guide me, to create my life from here forward, to make a difference in people's lives from my little corner of the world.

Always remember, never give up on life!

For more information

www.anniebaatz.com

www.facebook.com/AnnieBaatz1

www.instagram.com/anniebaatz

www.facebook.com/groups/PowerfulPositiveThoughtPatterns/

Hearts to be Heard

Giving a Voice to Creativity!

Wouldn't you love to help the physically, spiritually, and mentally challenged?

Would you like to make a difference in a child's life?

Imagine giving them:
confidence; self-esteem; pride; and self-respect.
Perhaps a legacy that lives on.

You see, that's what we do.
We give a voice to the creativity in their hearts,
for those who would otherwise not be heard.

Join us by going to

HeartstobeHeard.com

Help us, help others.

Made in the USA
Monee, IL
05 December 2020